KILLER CATS

PUMAS

By Wade Karlin

Gareth Stevens
Publishing

Please visit our website, www.garethstevens.com. For a free color catalog of all our high-quality books, call toll free 1-800-542-2595 or fax 1-877-542-2596.

Library of Congress Cataloging-in-Publication Data

Karlin, Wade.
Pumas / Wade Karlin.
   p. cm. — (Killer cats)
Includes index.
ISBN 978-1-4339-7012-2 (pbk.)
ISBN 978-1-4339-7013-9 (6-pack)
ISBN 978-1-4339-7011-5 (library binding)
1. Puma—Juvenile literature. I. Title.
QL737.C23K386 2012
599.75′24—dc23

                        2011044272

First Edition

Published in 2013 by
Gareth Stevens Publishing
111 East 14th Street, Suite 349
New York, NY 10003

Designer: Daniel Hosek
Editor: Therese Shea

Photo credits: Cover, all backgrounds, pp. 1, 5, 7, 8–9, 11, 13, 15, 17, 21 Shutterstock. com;
p. 19 Daniel Cox/Oxford Scientific/Getty Images.

Printed in the United States of America

CPSIA compliance information: Batch #CS12GS: For further information contact Gareth Stevens, New York, New York at 1-800-542-2595.

Contents

Boldface words appear in the glossary.

Many Names

Have you heard of mountain lions? Pumas? What about cougars? Catamounts? You might be surprised to learn that they're all the same animal! However, scientists usually call these big cats pumas.

Pumas have so many names because they live in so many places. They can be found from Canada to South America, though they're not often found in eastern parts of Canada and the United States. Pumas call many kinds of **habitats** home, including mountains, deserts, forests, grasslands, and swamps.

THAT'S WILD!

"Panther" is a name used for any big cat with a solid coat color. Pumas are sometimes called panthers, too.

The name "puma" comes from the Inca language.

Sizing Up the Puma

The puma has a long body. It can grow to be 5 feet (1.5 m) or more in length. Its tail may add another 3 feet (90 cm). A puma has a small head and small, round ears. Male pumas can weigh as much as 220 pounds (100 kg). Females are usually smaller and weigh less than males.

A puma's coat may be gray, reddish, or a brownish yellow. The tip of its tail and top of its ears are black. The throat, belly, and insides of the legs are white.

THAT'S WILD!

Pumas are the second-largest cat in the Americas. Only the jaguar is larger.

A puma has black fur around its nose and mouth, or its muzzle.

Ambush!

Like other big cats, pumas are born to hunt. They have large paws and long claws for bringing down **prey**. They have strong, powerful back legs that help them jump far. Pumas can also run very fast. Like cheetahs, pumas have a bendable backbone, or spine, so they can make quick turns while running.

However, pumas mostly like to keep hidden as they hunt. Then they **ambush** their prey! They leap on the animal and knock it to the ground. They can kill with a single bite.

Pumas are incredible jumpers. Some can jump as far as 40 feet (12 m)!

What's to Eat?

Pumas usually hunt between sundown and sunrise. The dark of the night helps them stay hidden as they follow, or stalk, their prey.

Pumas hunt creatures large and small, including deer, sheep, rabbits, wild pigs, raccoons, hares, moose, mice, and squirrels. After killing a large animal, a puma may drag it to a safe place. Then it buries its prey under leaves or grass so it can come back and eat for several days after the hunt.

THAT'S WILD!

Pumas can eat porcupines without being harmed by their **quills!**

Pumas live about 12 years in the wild and up to 25 years in zoos.

11

Home Ranges

Like some other big cats, pumas like to live alone in large **territories** called "home ranges." This way, they don't have to share prey with other pumas. Pumas know each other's ranges by signs they leave behind, such as scratches on trees and in the ground. They also leave their waste so other pumas smell it and know to stay away!

Male pumas have larger home ranges than females do. Male territories overlap with several female territories. Males choose these females as **mates**.

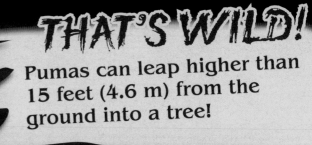

THAT'S WILD!

Pumas can leap higher than 15 feet (4.6 m) from the ground into a tree!

When pumas want to rest or hide from bad weather, they look for a cave or some bushes to hide under.

13

Puma Babies

When a female puma is ready to have babies, she looks for a den to keep them safe. She may have one to six babies at a time. The babies are called cubs or kittens. The mother keeps them in the den until they're old enough to follow her, around the age of 6 months.

Mothers **protect** their cubs from male pumas, who may kill them so the mother will mate again. Cubs stay with their mothers for up to 2 years. Females usually give birth every other year.

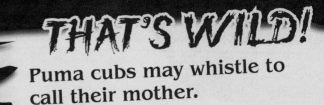

THAT'S WILD!

Puma cubs may whistle to call their mother.

Puma cubs have dark spots that disappear by the time they're 14 weeks old.

15

Pumas and People

People have hunted pumas for many years for sport as well as to keep pumas from eating their livestock. Pumas aren't seen often on the East Coast anymore because they were hunted so much. In addition, pumas need large territories and can't live in populated areas.

Why does the disappearance of pumas matter? Pumas are an important part of their **food web**. They eat sick and old animals. They also keep down the numbers of other animals. Without pumas, their habitat loses its balance.

THAT'S WILD!

Today, there are about 30,000 pumas left in the United States.

Some kinds of pumas are protected by laws now so that they don't disappear forever.

17

The Florida Panther

The Florida panther is a puma that once lived as far west as Texas and as far north as Tennessee. However, people hunted them until there were very few remaining. This puma is only found in the thick forests of southern Florida today. There are fewer than 100 Florida panthers left.

Though Florida panthers are now protected, it will be hard for their population to come back. They're less likely to find mates than other pumas and are dealing with **disease**, too.

Some Florida panthers may be seen in Everglades National Park.

19

Puma Protection

Pumas do harm people but not very often. They would usually rather avoid them. When pumas attack people, it's because the cats mistake them for prey.

There are several things people can do to keep themselves safe from pumas. The most important tip is never walk alone in places where pumas may live. People also shouldn't feed wild animals or leave food near campsites. Last, if a person does come in contact with a puma, they shouldn't run but should try to scare it away or fight back.

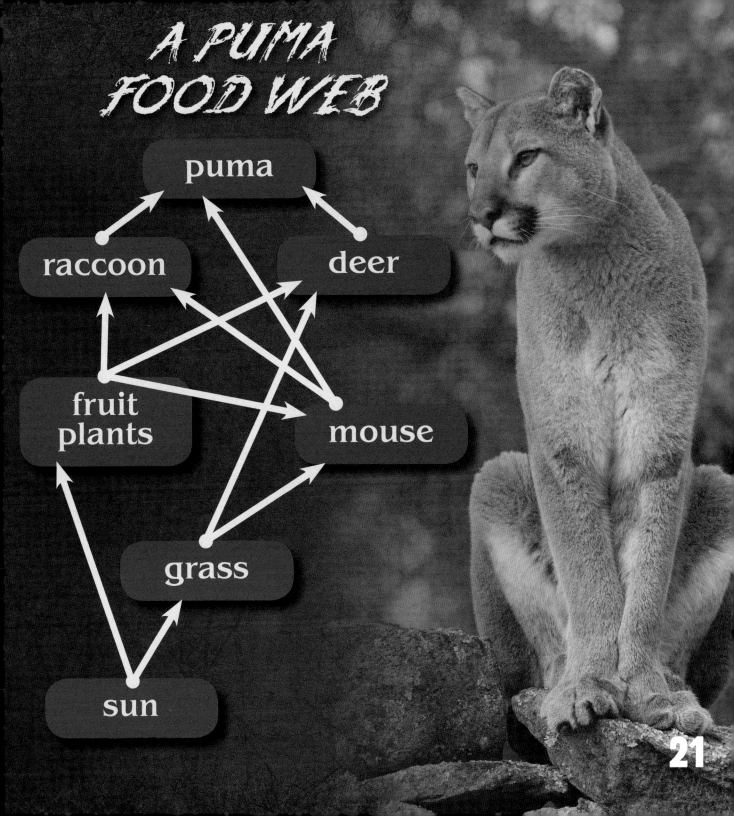

A PUMA FOOD WEB

puma

raccoon

deer

fruit plants

mouse

grass

sun

Glossary

ambush: an unexpected attack from a hidden place

disease: illness

food web: the way in which animals and plants pass energy within a community

habitat: an area where plants, animals, and other living things live

mate: one of two animals that come together to make babies. Also, to come together to make babies.

prey: an animal that is hunted by other animals for food

protect: to guard

quill: a sharp, stiff point on the body of an animal

territory: an area of land that an animal lives in and guards

For More Information

BOOKS

Markle, Sandra. *Mountain Lions.* Minneapolis, MN: Lerner Publications, 2010.

Rake, Jody Sullivan. *Pumas: On the Hunt.* Mankato, MN: Capstone Press, 2010.

Rodriguez, Cindy. *Cougars.* Vero Beach, FL: Rourke Publishing, 2009.

WEBSITES

Mammals: Mountain Lion (Pumas, Cougars)
www.sandiegozoo.org/animalbytes/t-puma.html
Read much more about this many-named big cat.

Mountain Lion
animals.nationalgeographic.com/animals/mammals/mountain-lion/
Hear what these big cats sound like.

Index